POEMS OF THE
TWO CENTURIES

POEMS OF THE TWO CENTURIES

Zukisani (Zuki) Maraqana

authorHOUSE®

AuthorHouse™
1663 Liberty Drive
Bloomington, IN 47403
www.authorhouse.com
Phone: 1-800-839-8640

First published by AuthorHouse   08/29/2011

ISBN: 978-1-4567-9726-3 (sc)
ISBN: 978-1-4567-9727-0 (ebk)

Printed in the United States of America

Any people depicted in stock imagery provided by Thinkstock are models,
and such images are being used for illustrative purposes only.
Certain stock imagery © Thinkstock.

This book is printed on acid-free paper.

Because of the dynamic nature of the Internet, any web addresses or links
contained in this book may have changed since publication and may no longer be
valid. The views expressed in this work are solely those of the author and do not
necessarily reflect the views of the publisher, and the publisher hereby disclaims
any responsibility for them.

Contents

WHERE SHEPHERDS JOY

'tis 'pon these Umlongo hills,
A taste of this planet, and of heaven,
Where shepherds joy;
Near tribulation, near comfort;
Pastures green, skies blue and longing lungs.

'tis on streaming valleys 'f this mount,
Where shepherds pride;
A shoal of family finned,
An assured catch for the novice bait;
A county's ease for the thirsty and languid.

'tis Airs from the neighbourhood winged,
A sonata of larks and cuckoo;
A natural menuet and concerto;
A sured shame for the Orchestra of Dura,
Plains of Babylon of old.

'tis 'pon these mounts and surrounds,
Where shepherds joy,
A scenery that sculpts morrow's bards great;
A moment of mourn and sorrow,
As shepherds homeward head.

By Zukisani Zuki(nickname) Maraqana

I SMILED

I smiled,
Beneath the cushion of repeated blankets,
Through the nights at their up-most turn,
As the brightened beam beamed through,
To bend for e'er my bleakened past.

I smiled,
At the advancement of dawn,
To see the massive torch of the firmament,
Retreating to its cocoon of old,
Shy of the beauty 'bandoned by Devine.

I smiled,
At the voice like the harp strings nigh,
The pearly set seldom seen, yet sweet,
The countenance of charm,
And the balls of light shy, yet wisely beholding.

I smiled,
At the touch that induced the lifely move,
The wanting fountains on the leeward side,
The eyelids lashing with calm,
And the rosy petals that despise the time.

By Zukisani Maraqana

THE EARLY WINTER MORN

'tis early winter morn,
Hear the trembling engines,
Amidst the shifting cock-crows;
Up in the firmament, the early star,
Stubborn, when all the way, broad,
Has been cleansed, from milk spilt;
To lighten abroad,
The journey of the night wanderer.

The veil of purity,
Half-made and done,
Unearth in part,
The once green countenance,
Now dreary and scarred,
By the impatient Autumn,
And streams of the panorama,
Reluctant to dance, but till sunshine.

Far and nigh,
The half-faint figure,
Advance, but yet come,
Humped with the cursed blessing,
Burdened, now one times two,
Times now altogether changed,
Infants awake for kindergarten,
As mothers rush to sell their toil.

The giant star,
Red like a Welder's rod,
Untamed, by the passion,
Deep, and blue;
The last warning now,
To wake the indolent and lazy;
'tis dawn, 'tis a new day,
Time to dine thy boiling brow.

By Zukisani Maraqana

THE RAND AT MORN

I watched the sun rise,
And the ice melting ere my eyes,
The bouquet, dew-fresh,
Unearthing its brightened beauty.

I watched the mine dunes,
Brown and golden at peak,
Like a stone of utmost purity,
Buried deep in its bowels.

I watched the revving toys many,
Henry Ford's dream fulfilled,
In defiance of mileage regulated,
Marking the start of a day's toil.

I watched the motored millipede,
Puffing on its perfect path,
As Commuters wind work-ward,
For the farthing and for the penny.

By Zukisani Maraqana

THE PEBBLES

Eggs of nature,
Half buried in mortar,
Some round, and some oblong,
Miles away from seas of birth.

Deprived of locomotion free,
In dozens and scattered they lay,
Divorced from siblings other,
And separated from kinsmen.

Behold some stock-piled,
In the landscaper's yard,
Forced to move a hundred yard away,
Like the slaves of old for the new world.

Eggs of nature,
Half buried and submerged,
Some brown and some grey,
Miles away from the seas of birth.

Conceived in the belly,
Of mothers, light years passed on,
Carved from immerse rocks,
Silt now in seas deep and ore.

By Zukisani Maraqana

YIELD ME NOT

Yield me not my abandoned flesh,
Beneath the sand and stone heap,
When my soul neither fresh,
Up yonder hast gone, and in leap,
For I will but partly rest,
And thy reason listen, but merely as jest.

Yield me not amongst habitations,
Despised, mean and colossal,
When I had well the revelations,
Of upper places well lit and ne'er brutal,
For I will, as nocturne bad,
Haunt you in days all, with omens sad.

Yield me not in rand my weary bones,
In wilderness with neither phones,
For the men of wealth will come,
To shake me in the underworld.
To save a farthing and a pound.

Yield not the life wanting me
Not in wilderness with neither phones,
For the underworld shall ne'er be sound,
Burry me in sepulcres of my forebears,
To be called and wake for immortal years.

By Zukisani Maraqana

BEYOND THOSE MOUINTAINS

Beyond those mountains,
There is a maiden I love,
My heart would wonder and wander,
'sif in my dreams her shalt see.

The neighborhood here 'gainst I frown,
The bouquet around not as bright,
Pearls and pebbles not as pleasing,
For the maiden royal is neither on sight.

Beyond those mountains,
There is a maiden I love,
My heart would wonder and wander,
'sif in my dreams her shalt see.

By Zukisani Maraqana

THE PERIOD APART

The bird of steel took off,
Battled beyond the blazing ball,
My light beamed,
Until it beamed no more.

An eagle of iron,
And ten-scores of lives in her bowels,
And far below, a zig-zag of paths minute,
And river meandering its ways towards the sea,

A thousand mile away she was,
The hi and lo mounts blurred the way,
The mist and cloud, and fog and dews,
Sporadic all, blocked the view.

The week long was a bygone,
At time same watch the sun,
And at time same watch the moon,
Yet by chance for eyes together.

Sweet in tongue 's in speech,
Compliant with the word, 's in custom,
Beam bright eyes, gift most eternal,
Yet when the eagle lands, shall I be.

By Zukisani Maraqana

COUNTIES OF HIS MAJESTY

They stretch forth,
From Tugela to Umzimvubu,
Golden crystals strewn across the coastline,
They widen deep, and leave the seas.

The sheep white, brave the passion, blue,
Swim along, t'wards the shore,
And waters shallow,
Drown the death unrevised.

The hills on shoreline, green,
Balls down scattered and perforated,
A sign of fuming nature,
Seventeen billion years ago.

The cool shadows of Sajonisi,
The man lone underneath, 'she rests,
The waves retreating Indiawards,
Beautiful art majestic fountains.

By Zukisani Maraqana

THE WILDERNESS
OF THE KAROO

The wilderness of the Karoo,
With its dwarfish green and thorn,
The brightened bouquet of the Namas,
The desert that stretched to eternity,
The sea of the mighty dry lands.

The ox of the plough,
And the cow that chew the chud,
The calf that milks from behind,
The duck that despised the altitude,
To save its young from the merciless claws.

By Zukisani Maraqana

LIFE IS LOST

A shot was fired,
He fell on the ground,
To be seen, and heard of no more.

The sound of freedom was nigh,
And neither far were ululations,
Lo, a precious life was lost.

A shot was fired,
He fell into the ground,
To be seen and heard of no more.

By Zukisani Maraqana

THE DEATH

I saw it,
Flapping its wings,
Mild and moderate,
Mucus fluid from its beak
Eyes closing partly,
Yet in praise none,
And in exultation neither,
'twas a dove, or a pigeon?

Insects up, around and about,
Some touching its mouth,
The consumer with keen not,
Some birds fly,
And some cuckoo,
Where she is, struggle to live,
Her time tickling to extinction.

I saw her,
Flapping its wings,
A call made up yonder,

A date was set, by devine,
How sad, yet real,
She closed her eyes,
And she was no more.
By Zukisani Maraqana

O' WOUND UNCURED

O' wound uncured,
Come neither nigh to me,
For here lieth Busi Mhlongo,
And countless thousands, with neither the hope.

A butterfly of the stage,
An African songbird of rage,
That denied neither her linguistic birth,
To live foreign in her land.

Active on Shakespearean platform,
'she owns the atmosphere, hers,
An audience of whisper, deprived,
'she, for e'er sings.

O' wound uncured,
Come neither nigh to me,
For great diva here lieth,
Motionless, still and no more.

By Zukisani Maraqana

O' SLUMBER, SWEET SLUMBER

O' slumber, sweet slumber,
Why leaveth me from thee,
Amidst the dusk to crawl,
Through der Merwe's light clear,
To leave this my wife,
Beautiful and holy in her slumber.

The holy man hast just praised,
Birds of the night,
In cry but neither the cocks,
Ere the Angelic watch,
Ere the mentis of pray,
To beat the dust, ere the dawn,

Times were there,
For me hast I done,
Left the home, ere the star of morn,
For the stage of slumber,
Icy hands the night through,
Motionless in life, the nasal drums.

None now but thee,
But thou, sayeth, "haste thyself,"
O' slumber, sweet slumber,
Why leaveth me from thee,
I will, though will be nil,
And beat the dust to wait the toil.

By Zukisani Maraqana

SHALL I SEIZE TO BE

Shall I seize to be,
In the manner of things all,
And my eyes for e' er close,
To see the landscape no more.

Shall I seize to be,
And be on the earth no more,
And feel the feeling I felt,
Ere the universe forth was given.

Shall I seize to be,
And be in darkest place ne'er known,
Like Berlioz in symphonie fantastique,
Hell then to have me shall giggle.

Shall I seize to be,
And at trumpet last shall I rise,
And up heavenward with Angelic flight,
Unto the bosom of Melchizedek.

By Zukisani Maraqana

REJOICE GREATLY

Rejoice greatly,
And walk tall stately,
For now thy land is the battle field,
And though lost is thy shield.

The nations all in thy soil converged,
By thy God's might, victory has emerged,
To light this continent gloriously,
Though few were bitter, furiously.

Why art thou lame?
And one loss left you shame?
This cup was surely not thine,
And it shall, for other nation shine.

Calleth thou a small thing,
That to us hast come, the ring?
This shield is neither thine for sure,
And by creation is meant for other shore.

Why lamentest thou and them?
For in thy soil is Sham and Ham,

Like the middle eleven upon the least,
And in multitudes, unceast.

Rejoice, Africa, rejoice,
And call upon thy God, with neither choice,
For He looked upon thy plight,
And remembered us, upon His sight.

For like Macabeus thou hast fought,
Against thee were all fire balls shot,
The battle was heavy, thou had to fall,
And thou were nobled in thy glorious fall.

By Zukisani Maraqana
For SA FIFA world cup.

O' STAR BLACK

O' star, black,
What did thou lack?
That now faded is thy star,
And thy light reachest not the Tsar.

O' black star,
Thy could not reach far,
And thy could brighten no longer,
And the giants about thee were stronger.

Hope of all Africans,
Thou hast shivered great Tuscans,
And neither hast thou down t'wards the deck,
To disgrace us, many from the shack.

The decade is new, thou wilt shine,
And the century tender, we shall all dine,
The crown golden, shall we lift,
For God justified, shall he not sift.

By Zukisani Maraqana

(Poems of the FIFA World cup SA 2010)

THE PRE-MAN LIGHT YEARS

The fumes, deep and dark, as midnight,
The unformed earth, buried under the seas,
The cracking sounds of the big bang,
As forces fought, 'sif never to end,
The deafening and rumbling thunder,
And the lightening, to blind the beholder.

Life in pre-Angelic times,
Potentially unbearable for every and all,
The Spirit of the lone,
And most High raged,
The mighty hand steered alone,
And the power Devine reigned, and in solitude.

Times too premature for any creature,
Period itself at stage of pre-nature,
Who could have stood,
For times then were very rude,

Forces calm and be good,
All be still, and know that I AM God.

By Zukisani Maraqana
(Poems of pre-creation)

TAKE ME NOT FROM THIS COUNTRY

Take me not from this country,
Even though it lacks many a foundry,
Yet I dare not live our fountains,
That with pride floweth, from our mountains.

Take me not from this land,
And move me from our golden sand,
A natural seam of seas and its shores,
A poor man's entitlement to shares.

Allow me not to leave these meadows,
And take me from sight of its willows,
For I will not see these bovines in peace,
With young ones in hygienic kiss.

Can I go away?
I will surely be astray,
For wonderful are the works of the most High,
That lives the lone Sojourner to sigh.

By Zukisani Maraqana
(From the pastoral poems)

ANOTHER VICTIM

Once a queen of the catwalk,
Once a princess of the brothel,
And now she lies,
Her sun has set,
Ere the age of maturity,
A bottle of Atlantas' beverage is no more.

She lies there motionless,
Neither the lone audience,
'Sir Verdi's opera of ball,
And midweek with few mourners,
With earths' mouth wide to swallow'
Like the hippo of great lakes central.

Bones of number, twenty scores and fourteen,
In folds of the resistant wrap,
And a dog-collar by the graveside waits,
To undo this creation'
The way heavenward very differential,
And all are bound to follow her heels.

By Zukisani Maraqana

THE BEAUTY OF
THE CREATION

Behold, the waters, blue in the great seas,
And in closer proximity,
Changes its colour, like a chameleon,
Lo in Sabie, the Berlin falls,
Stepping in its falls,
Length of my life, a two score and eight,
Its lifely fluid towards the oceans.

Mountain here, and mountain there,
Mpumalanga, a Lowveld most gifted,
Greater Moholo-holo, a throne of the Almighty,
Where fierce battles were fought,
Between the Pedis and the Swazis,
Pedis on top, throwing stones,
Climb for Swazis 'gainst ability, faced defeat.

The Sudwala caves, oldest in the world,
Of three thousand million years of life,
Eleven metre height of ventilated space,
A sanctuary of chief Somquba,

A ceiling of two thousand million years of fossilized algae,
An unexplored scenery of thirty-four kilometers,
That twines the towns of Mbombela and Mashishing.

The scenery of the Tsitsikama,
With beautiful valleys of the diverse flora,
Stretches themselves towards the blue sea,
The Bloukrans bridge, though man made,
The world's highest bungy jump,
And the waterfalls of the Tsitsikama,
Puffing through the rocky cliffs, to meet the seas.

By Zukisani Maraqana

O' THE MIDNIGHT BEAUTY

May I bid thee night,
To let the brightened beauty pass,
And 'llow thy flashing eyes,
To escape from me.

Through the night deep,
And arms in concord heavenward,
Brightness that despise the depth of darkness,
And countenance beaming.

O' lady fair,
Fly not and escape my sight,
For thy perfume fly fine,
And for e'er is the sight of thy smile.

By Zukisani Maraqana

I WATCHED WITH GRIEF

I watched with grief,
When charming valleys were not mine,
Very far was the relief,
As gems own for the Alliens did shine.

I watched with grief,
As waters mine by rivals were drunk,
And my neck stood stiff,
As shafts on mines were sunk.

I watched with grief,
As sheep mine land in someone's kraal,
I watched hidden behind the cliff,
And saw the Uitlanders stroll.

I watched with grief,
As cows mine were milked,
And the yield taken to the reef,
As shepherds lives were at risk.

By Zukisani Maraqana

THE LANDSCAPES OF OUR KINGS

The great Drakensberg,
A chain of the Almighty,
's He beholds His sons
The Kings, and smile,
Over his virgin maidens,
To bless the fields with rain,
The valleys of the Amajuba hills.

The dews of fresh plains of the Pondoland,
The great mounts doing the skeil,
The goat standing on hind,
To reach the tender leaves,
The chick of the eagle,
Staggering as they learn to fly,
Protected by the heights.

By Zukisani Maraqana

THIS BODY IS NOT MINE

This body is not mine,
And cannot be the replica mine;
The fake me cannot even swallow,
The copied me shakes in wind, like a willow;
Take away this thing,
For wert me, wert to sing.

This body is not mine,
For wert mine, wert to dine,
Sure-footed, like a goat, mine is,
And not old and frail it is,
Mine are not these mountains of pimples,
Mine neither, are these valleys of wrinkles.

This body is not mine,
For this fake's hour does not shine,
Lo the bones, gathered in the bundle,
In thy state, why not grumble,
Time for sure is come,
The same had been, with some.

By Zukisani Maraqana

OUR GREAT
WATER-FALLS

The Angel Salto water-falls,
Taking short of a kilometer in drop,
Wharfing and fuming in its terrain,
Roars to wipe into abyss,
Every and all in its path,
The glittering python of Venezuelan Highlands.

The Tugela-falls,
Stands tall in its space own,
Two eight four thousand feet in length,
A pride of the African soil,
Has only but one king to hail,
Far in the Latin American counties.

The Ankoerebis-falls of the Orange,
With its rumbling and deafening noise,
Stands high for two hundred and forty metres,
In a barren and desolate stretches of sand,
In land once the kingdom of the Khoikhoi,
It stretches eighteen kilometers into the Atlantic.

The mighty Berlin-falls, fifty and hundred metres,
Ambience displayed on the panorama,
Run and rush through the wooden grasslands,
It starts mean and despised in its top,
Widening at the bottom from the self-made pool,
Like the candle light turned upside-down.

The Horwick water-falls,
Of height ninety three metres,
Meanders with the meandering midlands,
A scenery beloved by the journey men,
And its waters crystal and clear,
Travel a hundred kilometers into the ocean.

The Micmac-falls on the panorama,
A length of metres, four and sixty,
Can neither be forgotten nor sidelined,
The Lisbon-falls of Mpumalanga, stands ninety and
two metres,
And who dares not mention the Niagara-falls,
That spans the cities of York and Ontario.

By: Zukisani Maraqana

SMILE FOR EVERY CREATURE

Smile for every creature, smile,
For the cat that breathes, with moistened claw,
For the rat of the hole,
That limits its outing,
For fear of consumption unbearable.

Smile, for every creature, smile,
For the small bird of the firmament,
That fly heavenward,
In the blazing and visible heat,
Yet in its invisible size, the young cometh not short.

Smile, for every creature, smile,
For the blue crane of the wetlands,
A prideous display of our nation,
The eagle that flies swift, like the hawk of combat,
The hornbill of the yellow beak, about to varnish.

Smile, for every creature, smile,
The apes of the descending cliffs,
Red and hurt on their rear side,

That reluctantly climb, on landscape incline,
And carry the young, on back or belly.

Smile, while you can, smile,
And behold every bit of creation,
For time tick, and time tickles,
For where the man doeth his works,
All things bright shall be there no more.

By Zukisani Maraqana

'TIS A PITY THOU LEAVEST

'tis a pity thou leavest,
Ere thy services were 'ccomplished;
Or 'sit pastures out greener,
To leave this toil for other?

When place left exalted shall be,
Shall we thee behold?
O worthiness unseen,
For value gone, shall we lament.

Patriot in youth;
Surprise be mine,
Thou knowest the route,
And the direction be thine.

Which Cinderella,
The shoe thine shall wear?
West horizon et East,
None shall ever triumph.

Fare you well;
The blessing be thine;
But as thou beholdest, the highway be smooth,
Prithee comest thou, and labor on.

By Zukisani Maraqana

EXTEND THY HOUSE

Extend thy house,
And widen its walls,
Doth thou knowest,
Thou woman most precious,
That to thee refereth these words wise?

The Grand Architect hath planned,
Shall thou not build?
Survey and behold the neonate,
From its whence and thithers,
Was not it Japhtha, of whence same,
Yet with blessing of time,
Over house of Gilead all?

Perfume of paradise, heavenly most,
May nothing that flieth, impure,
Spoil the melody of thy scent,
Thou art a pebble of shore-line most splendid,
Carved to shape that I now behold,
By the Mighty hands,
Self, of the Lord Most High.

By: Zukisani Maraqana

THE TABERNACLE

It stands there stable and firm,
A splendid display of design triumph,
All these years, weather raging,
With neither the Designer's sketches,
And material quantities not known of old,
Cheaper in tariffs, fit for purpose.

Thick and deep by year
Is plaster, with skills, from within,
Neither the yardsticks were used,
And Engineer there was none,
Yet dominant feathers of science of numbers,
In its belly, the grandmother sits,

By the heath of the fire-wood, half-burnt,
Now twinkling towards slumber,
And a host of sons and daughters,
With a dozen times three grand offspring,
All fed from the incentives of age.

The oil-lamp, blinking,

The grindstone,

With day's work concluded,

Is now at rest.

The breast harp, and its bow,

And the finale of ultimate nocturne,

Retires the family to deep slumber,

Until the grandmother her-self,

The lyrics did she mumble, 'she sleeps

To waken by the first-crows.

By: Zukisani Maraqana

O' THE MAURITIAN WORLD

The waters of Mauritius,
Shallow and still,
Wanting in wave and in gull,
Where fishermen fish,
With no fright of the predator of the seas.

Ile aux Cerfs and its seas,
An island of activity and fun,
The boats are rowed,
The seas are guarded,
And in its shores, the banana of the desert.

See thyself, in the isle of coco,
Where settlers master the sail,
Mouth-watering dishes of the dry-land,
Potjiekos and the dumpling keep reminding,
South Africa, away from home.

By Zukisani Maraqana

SLEEP O' LASS, SLEEP

Sleep o' lass, sleep,
And slumber, o' lady fair,
But knowest as thou sleepest,
And comprehend as thou wakest,
That my heart lovest thee.

Nails of thine fingers,
And toes of thine feet,
The hair of thine cranium,
The ear twice, layeth on thy countenance,
All mine, that is thine.

Sleep o' lass, sleep,
And slumber o' lady fair,
But knowest as thou sleepest,
And comprehend as thou wakest,
That my heart lovest thee.

By: Zukisani Maraqana

THE CONTRA-PUNTAL DAYS

O' great days,
That today art no more,
Days of the Handel great,
Days of the counterpoint,
Lengthy period of fugue
In the seventeenth century they were.

Shakespeare for sure was artistic,
But bedded more in art is music,
I would hum the opera,
I would mimic the continuo,
But as many as they were,
Bards opera all cannot be memorized.

O' great days,
Days of Bach great,
A virtuoso of polyphony,
But hear this gift in Brandenburg one,

And this artistic excellence,
In cantata one plus fifty.

O' great days,
Days of concerti grossi,
Could I forget thee,
Musical pedagogist of Cologne,
A fine violinist of yore,
Arch-angelic in touch was Correlli.

O' great days of menuet,
And days of sonata of lute,
O' days of the harpsichord,
Come and drown my ears,
And though sun was set for baroque,
Mozart senior was to bridge the times.

By: Zukisani Maraqana

O' DAYS GONE PAST

O' days gone past,
Ye joyous days of yore,
How much I long for thee,
Mayest thou come to fill my heart.

When thee I calleth to mind,
My heart would start to wonder,
Like the hart wild,
In search of the fountain.

Why hast thou left me,
Why hast thou forsaken me,
Come again, sweet love,
And for e'er shalt we stay.

By: Zukisani Maraqana

O' ART, AN IMMORTAL ART

O' art, an immortal art,
Art that outlives its creator,
Light years after the note worthy death,
Art unto which we behold.

Lo the portrait of the giraffe,
Somewhat a horse, somewhat a lengthy goat,
Legs astride to quench her thirst,
Market-price, a thousand-fold more.

Survey the zebra,
Artistic in its nature,
Forever there,
In its canvas of eternity.

O' art, perfect art,
Art that for e'er breathes,
Albeit hast offspring its passage,
Art there for e'er shall live.

By: Zukisani Maraqana

HOW SHALL I SHOW THEE MY LOVE?

How shall I show thee my love?
With flowers from the garden?
Nay, for this the garden is thine,
And thou in it hast grossly labored.

How shall I show thee my love?
From petals and anthers of the veld?
Nay, for the Gardener is the Lord Almighty,
And maintenance thereof is from on High.

How shall I show thee my love?
From the bouquet of the florist stalls?
Nay, for the choice is neither mine,
And the labourer had it selected and graded.

How shall I show thee my love?
From the blossomed product self mine?
Nay, for though I have planted and watered,
The Lord on High hast made it to grow.

How shall I show thee my love?
From the refined work of gold and pearls?
Nay, for mines all and seas,
Are the works of God's creation.

How shall I show thee my love?
By helping thee, as thou troddest this earth?
To go heavenward, to get thy award?
Yea, trod with thee, to meet thy creator.

By: Zukisani Maraqana

THE JOURNEY OF A MADMAN

'tis his everyday routine,
Flower on the nose, most times withered,
And hat of ages on his head,
At intersections, a motor-man he is,
He moves and misses no time,
A baggage not compulsory, and plastic same.

'tis his curse of eternity,
To travel unrequired, unforced,
Along the em one route,
Through the vehicles speeding,
Yet no narrow shave,
Yet no narrow escape.

He starts at dawn,
And sets with the sun,
He marches on, a duet time,
And like Beethoven's dynamics,
At times very loud,
And sometimes abruptly soft.

All summer goes, all winter comes,

And people all, for vaccines called,

For him above the Physician is He,

He eats his food, with Pasteur none,

The food he keeps, with self the bin,

And systems all, for him a cure.

'tis his everyday routine,

Flower on his nose, often times withered,

And hat of ages on his head,

Valleys unwatered in his heels,

But as people rest, when will he?

On eternal rest, with trumpet sound.

By: Zukisani Maraqana

WHY CALLETH ME AN AFRICAN?

Why calleth me an African?
When the ocre of ancestry is at Wall street,
And the dress of loins only in museums found,
When virgins of my fatherland,
Are deemed nude, when in right-sized aprons.

Why calleth me an African?
When robes of my forefathers,
Are long done away with,
To give way to wear of teachers,
And those converted into sermon.

Why calleth me an African?
When food with chaff, healthy,
Has been seen as sign of illiteracy,
Yet from these soils of Africa,
Science of solutions did come.

Why calleth me an African?
When children mine from rooms many,

Talk to me with twisted toungues,
To despise the language to which we're born,
To look down on symbol of identity.

By: Zukisani Maraqana

WHY SMILETH EYE?

Why smileth eye?
At day-break, **and** at morn,
At dawn, and sunrise,
At time same, as star of morn,
For Christ He healed,
My sores and pains.

Why smileth eye?
As sun be set,
At even-tide,
At time of dusk,
For Christ He healed,
All torment is gone.

Why smileth eye?
This time of day,
As nite in midst
And wife in snore,
For Lord He came,
To save our souls.

By: Zukisani Maraqana

GREAT GREAT HEROES LIE

Great Ntu on other side of Zambesi lie,
A great forebear of Bantus all,
A great forefather of the Ngunis all,
And an ancestor to sons of Moyo,
He carried us from great-grandfather Ham,
And through him were we brought forth.

Great Tshawe by Umzimkhulu lies,
Minute in birth, 'sin stature,
Yet with immountable biceps,
Shook, like earthquake, the throne of Cirha,
Like Nimrod he was, and lacked fear,
And Tshangisa in his way stood not.

Great Hintsa by Umbhashe lies
His majesty, by Smith brutality, beheaded,
A man for peace he was,
And a traitor was he never,
Scores of Fingoes he welcomed,
And sorghum and milk sour did he give,

Great Cetshwayo by Umfolozi lies,
The gallant fighter of the Zulu lineage,
Well conversant with the sea of Islands,
He unceasantly fought to keep the crown,
Heroism of great magnitude had he,
And his blood, more sacred than Retief's.

By: Zukisani Maraqana

O' CREATION, GODLY CREATION

O' people all, behold the nature,
The skies above, and firmament therein,
At day the sun, and nite the moon,
The stars all, in galaxy and way,
And God alone, He did it all,
Praise be His, and might and all.

The flee unseen,
Its sting is felt,
The mosque of night,
Minute wings 'sit flies,
The violin it sounds,
The music be mute.

The locust of the field,
All crops be gone,
Abdomen in its grave,
Resurrection in millions,
O' people be still,
And know that He is God.

Lions of death,
To devour all men,
The tiny man stands,
To conquer it all,
The whale like ship,
Buried in God's seas.

The mountains climbing,
And the fountains descending,
The cliffs exulted,
And water-falls opposing,
All rivers of eels,
And lakes of calm.

The forest of rain,
And grain mass of drought,
The puffader burning,
In Namib sands,
God made it all 'lone,
And all praise be to Him.
Hallelujah!

By: Zukisani Maraqana

O' LIFE UNOURS

O' life unours,
For we are but owned all,
O' life ours borrowed,
And shalt from us recalled,
A constant reminder to us all,
That we shall by one called.

As we walk, shall we undo?
And as we wend, shall we unwend?
The journey we take, shall it return?
O' the stars heavenly doth know,
And heavens most firmamentic, likewise,
For Lord most High doth reign.

Take heed, o' mankind,
And be alert, o' sons of men,
Watch the lilies, at morn they brighten,
And at sunset, they fade,
A signal for sojourners all to survey,
For Lord most High doth reign.

By: Zukisani Maraqana

THE MIGHTIFUL SHALL REIGN

The Mightiful shall alone reign,
As leads all unstopped shall be,
To unleash the smelting potential,
All of buried furnaces,
To consume the highlands all,
Only the voice from on High.

The narrow paths and the highways,
The giant trees and the dwarfs,
The poor grass under foot-prints,
The walker that had it betrodden,
All with one flash of fire,
And all in no time shall disappear.

Mountains of stone below point freezing,
Mountains self, that incubate heat,
The valleys of extinction,
Both in drought and in flood,
Shall with rage of the Most Powerful,
In moment vanish, 'sif never were.

The wind of great might,
That destroyeth, 'sit advanceth,
No more shall it be,
The water of streams and of seas,
From above most catastrophic,
With wink of an eye, no more shall be.

Great Egypt, and great Babylon,
Mighty men of valour that abideth,
The gigantic Watusis of Rwanda,
And the Pygmies with courage great,
All of these shall dwindle,
From the host of the Heavenly army.

And when all nature is consumed,
And when the consumer itself is swallowed,
By the might of the Heavenly Father,
Then, the Almighty Three-fold shall stand,
When all is gone, and fury raging,
To reign alone, in glory by the Angelic host.

By: Zukisani Maraqana

TO WORK, TO WED, TO WEAR

I wake up, to work,
Ere the first cock crow,
'tis long this list,
'tis unending this journey,
At locomotives, with twisted jaws,
They greet, I nod, I snore.

The pennies, the farthing, I collect,
In the cash box, which,
Now and then I burgle,
The list is long, when to wed?
At toll of ages, the act doth change,
And in scroll, the revision neither.

At wedding, and before,
My uncle had toiled,
To part with euro,
To divorce from pounds,
At honeymoon I am called,
Why bursteth the pipe, and falleth the roof.

The time is gone,

No sight to retire,

My heir shall wait,

To receive in vain,

I came forth to sweat the brow,

To dine, to wed, to die at end.

By: Zukisani Maraqana